Anne Bradstreet

by Simonetta Carr

with Illustrations by Matt Abraxas

REFORMATION HERITAGE BOOKS
Grand Rapids, Michigan

Anne Bradstreet
© 2024 by Simonetta Carr

Cover artwork by Matt Abraxas
For additional artwork by Matt, see pages 7, 15, 21, 27, 29, 31, 37, 39, 41, 45, 47, 53.

All rights reserved. No part of this book may be used or reproduced in any manner whatsoever without written permission except in the case of brief quotations embodied in critical articles and reviews. Direct your requests to the publisher at the following addresses:

Reformation Heritage Books
3070 29th St. SE
Grand Rapids, MI 49512
616-977-0889
e-mail: orders@heritagebooks.org
website: www.heritagebooks.org

Printed in China
24 25 26 27 28/10 9 8 7 6 5 4 3 2 1

Library of Congress Cataloging-in-Publication Data

Names: Carr, Simonetta, author. | Abraxas, Matt, illustrator.
Title: Anne Bradstreet / by Simonetta Carr ; with illustrations by Matt Abraxas.
Description: Grand Rapids, Michigan : Reformation Heritage Books, 2024. | Series: Christian biographies for young readers
Identifiers: LCCN 2023056927 | ISBN 9798886861006 (hardcover)
Subjects: LCSH: Bradstreet, Anne, 1612?-1672—Juvenile literature. | Poets, American—Colonial period, ca. 1600-1775—Biography—Juvenile literature. | Puritans—Massachusetts—Biography—Juvenile literature. | LCGFT: Biographies.
Classification: LCC PS712 .C37 2024 | DDC 811/.1 [B]—dc23/eng/20231218
LC record available at https://lccn.loc.gov/2023056927

For additional Reformed literature, request a free book list from Reformation Heritage Books at the above address.

CHRISTIAN BIOGRAPHIES FOR YOUNG READERS

This series introduces children to important people in the Christian tradition. Parents and schoolteachers alike will welcome the excellent educational value it provides for students, while the quality of the publication and the artwork make each volume a keepsake for generations to come. Furthermore, the books in the series go beyond the simple story of someone's life by teaching young readers the historical and theological relevance of each character.

OTHER VOLUMES

John Calvin
Augustine of Hippo
John Owen
Athanasius
Lady Jane Grey
Anselm of Canterbury
John Knox
Jonathan Edwards
Marie Durand
Martin Luther
Peter Martyr Vermigli

Irenaeus
John Newton
Julia Gonzaga
B.B. Warfield
John Bunyan
Phillis Wheatley
Byang Kato
Charles Haddon Spurgeon
Patrick of Ireland
Wang Mingdao

Table of Contents

Introduction 5

Chapter 1: Growing and Learning 6

Chapter 2: A Brand-New World 17

Chapter 3: A Passion for Writing 25

Chapter 4: A Published Author 33

Chapter 5: Joys and Sorrows 40

Chapter 6: Leaving a Legacy 49

Time Line 55

Did You Know? 56

From Anne's Pen 61

Acknowledgments 63

ANNE BRADSTREET

Maps of places important to Anne Bradstreet's life in Old and New England.
You may want to use them to trace all her moves to new homes.

MAP CREATED BY TOM CARROLL

Introduction

Anne Bradstreet was the first published poet in America. She arrived from England in 1630, when the American continent was, to Europeans, different and challenging. In spite of the difficulties of a pioneering life and the disapproval of people who thought that only men should be writing and studying, Anne continued to express her thoughts and prayers in beautiful poetry.

Today, many people study her writings as interesting accounts of life in America's early colonies. They also appreciate that Anne described her life with honesty, relating both its struggles and joys. But for Christians, her poems are much more. They are an encouragement to recognize God's love and wisdom in the beauty of this world, in the strength and comfort He is faithful to provide, and most of all in His unfailing promises.

All images and portraits of Anne Bradstreet were made long after her death, so no one knows what she looked like. This image was made in the nineteenth century.

FRONTISPIECE FOR AN ACCOUNT OF ANNE BRADSTREET: THE PURITAN POETESS, AND KINDRED TOPICS, EDITED BY COLONEL LUTHER CALDWELL (1898)

CHAPTER ONE
Growing and Learning

Anne was born in March 1612 to a well-respected family in Northampton, a busy market town northwest of London. Her parents, Thomas and Dorothy Dudley, kept a good-sized library and valued education greatly. Thomas was known as "a devourer of books." As was common in those days, they sent their sons to school and taught their daughters at home.

The Bible had an important place in Anne's home. On Sundays the family went to church, where Anne listened carefully to the sermons. When she was about six or seven years old, she started to understand that disobedience to God, which the Bible calls sin, is a terrible offense to a loving heavenly Father. She tried hard not to sin, and when she did, she could not find peace until she confessed it to God. She also found much comfort in reading the Scriptures. "As I grew to have more understanding," she explained, "so the more solace [comfort] I took in them."

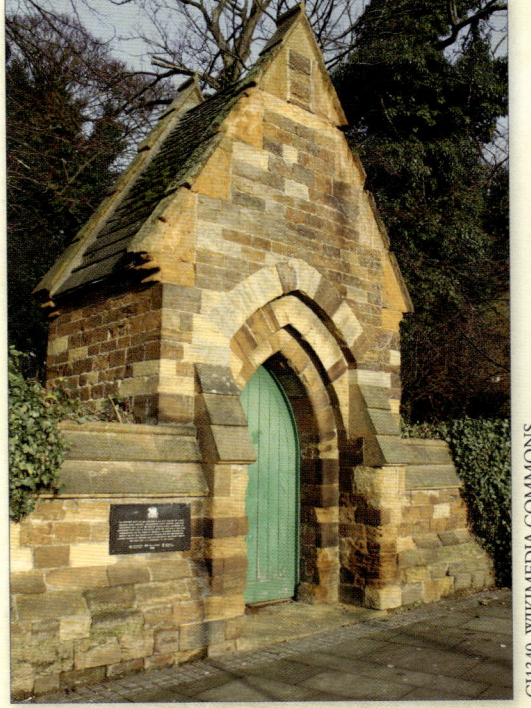

This gate is all that is left of the large castle built in Northampton in the eleventh century that was still standing when Anne was born.

Anne's parents provided her education at home.

GROWING AND LEARNING

7

In 1619 Lord Theophilus Clinton, fourth Earl of Lincoln, invited Thomas to work for him at his estate in Sempringham, about fifty miles northeast of Northampton. (An earl is a nobleman, equal in rank to a count.) At that time, the earl was only twenty years old and needed Thomas's help in taking care of his finances and correspondence. Thomas accepted. It was a good job and gave his family the opportunity to live with people who shared their religious convictions and love for education.

Coat of arms of the Clinton family (family symbol)

VATEGV, WIKIMEDIA COMMONS

The estate was made up of many buildings, with enough rooms for the earl's immediate and extended family, servants, and frequent guests. Anne was able to study with the same tutors the earl's family hired for their children. The estate's library, much larger than her family's, must have been one of Anne's favorite places.

Guillaume du Bartas was a French Protestant poet who had great influence on Anne. He wrote a long poem about the creation of the world and the history of humanity.

WIKIMEDIA COMMONS

Besides learning reading, writing, and the Scriptures, she would have studied history, math, science, and some languages that were useful at that time, such as Latin and French. She especially liked the poetry of a French author who was famous at that time, Guillaume du Bartas. Anne said she learned a lot by reading his poems.

By the time they arrived at Sempringham, seven-year-old Anne was already the oldest daughter in her family. Her sister Patience was four or five, and a new sister, Sarah, was soon to be born. Another sister, Mercy, would be born a year later. Anne was probably expected to teach her younger sisters the things she had learned.

St. Botolph's Church in Boston, Lincolnshire. With one of the tallest medieval towers in the country, it has been called the "Stump" from the time it was built.
STEVE, FLICKR

Lord Theophilus had a chapel in his estate where a local chaplain or a visiting pastor preached the gospel every Sunday. One of these visitors was John Cotton, pastor of St. Botolph's Church in Boston. The Dudleys appreciated Cotton's faithfulness in preaching the gospel truthfully and clearly and often traveled by wagon to Boston to hear him preach at his church. When they did, they would leave on Saturday and spend the night in one of the earl's Boston properties. In 1625 they moved to one of these estates and stayed there for about three years, still at the earl's service.

Around the end of their stay, an epidemic of smallpox ravaged the region. Smallpox is a contagious disease that causes high fever and the breakout of painful, small boils over the body. No cure or vaccination existed, and many people died. Anne caught smallpox soon after her move and had to stay in bed many months.

As most Christians do in difficult times, Anne prayed earnestly and asked God to forgive her sins. In her case, she was particularly sorry for losing interest in God's Word, which had started when she became a teenager. Thankfully, God healed her. Often, smallpox leaves marks on the skin, but we don't know if this happened to Anne. If it did, the marks would have reminded her of God's healing from this deadly illness.

She recovered in time for her wedding to her father's young assistant, Simon Bradstreet. At that time, most marriages were arranged by the families of the bride and groom, and Anne's marriage might have been planned for a while. In any case, she had plenty of time to get to know Simon, as he worked for her father for six years. At the time of their marriage, Simon was working for a noble family at Leez Priory in the county of Essex, so Anne moved there with him.

Leez Priory in Essex, where Simon Bradstreet worked for a while, belonged to the Earl of Warwick. The building has now been remodeled. Like the estate of the Earl of Lincoln, it was a beautiful and large place where Anne could continue to read and learn.

ANDY SCOTT, WIKIMEDIA COMMONS

William Laud

INTERNET BOOK ARCHIVE (FROM *THE HISTORY AND ANTIQUITIES, ANCIENT AND MODERN, OF THE BOROUGH OF READING, IN THE COUNTY OF BERKS*, 1816)

King Charles I

WELLCOME IMAGES

The young couple's happiness was only marred by growing concerns about the English church and government. For some time, many Christians in England had protested some ceremonies of the Church of England that reminded them of the Roman Catholic Church. Their concerns grew when William Laud, the man King Charles I had appointed as highest authority in the church under him, made these ceremonies mandatory and punished people who tried to avoid them. These opposing Christians were often known as Puritans because they wanted to purify the English church.

Besides these religious concerns, many people were also worried about the king's tendency to act without checking with Parliament, as English law required. These problems became particularly real to the Dudley family when Lord Theophilus was imprisoned in the Tower of London for opposing a law that demanded people give loans to the king.

Some Puritans, including Thomas Dudley, started to think it was time to leave England. They had a particular place in mind just north of Plymouth in North America, where other Europeans had founded a colony in 1620.

The Tower of London, a historic landmark in central London, England, was built as a fortress, a royal palace, and a prison.

A statue of John Winthrop in Boston, Massachusetts

Theophilus's daughter Arabella and her husband, Isaac Johnson, helped to finance a group of men who agreed to scout the region, clear the land, build homes, and plant crops—preparing the place for future travelers. The scouts' first report was encouraging. The land, they said, had fruit, fish, and other meat in abundance. After a while, however, they stopped sending reports. Their silence was concerning, but the travelers were still determined to go.

The preparations took time, but few people dared to sail before the summer anyway. In the meantime, there were properties to sell and many supplies to buy because there were no shops or markets in the New World. Thomas Dudley was voted deputy governor of the group, which meant he was second in command after John Winthrop, a well-respected lawyer. Simon agreed to serve as secretary. Finally, in March 1630, the Dudleys and the Bradstreets met with the other travelers in Southampton, ready to leave.

After long preparations, Anne and her husband were ready to leave England.

GROWING AND LEARNING

John Cotton
INTERNATIONAL ARCHIVE BOOK IMAGES

Anne and her family and friends traveled on the main ship, named Arabella after Arabella Johnson. Three other ships followed: the Talbot, the Ambrose, and the Jewell. Each could hold about three hundred people. Of these four, Arabella reached its destination first.

John Cotton surprised the group of travelers by riding to Southampton, despite his ill health, to preach a farewell sermon, comforting fearful hearts with the reminder that God would always be with them. Winthrop spoke next, urging everyone to stay united and mindful of each other both during the long journey and after their arrival. "For we must consider that we shall be as a city upon a hill," he said. "The eyes of all people are upon us." He warned them that if they didn't stay faithful to God, people all over the world would remember them as a sad story and a poor example.

CHAPTER TWO
A Brand-New World

Today, we might think of a trip across the ocean as an exciting adventure, but at that time it was extremely dangerous. There was always the possibility of a shipwreck or an encounter with pirates. Many travelers got sick on the way, especially those who stayed in crowded quarters.

Departing was also a heartbreaking occasion, because few people could afford to travel back and forth across the ocean, and most of the passengers knew they would never again see their beloved country and the many friends and family they were leaving behind. It was with these thoughts and many tears and prayers that the Puritans on the fleet left England on Easter Monday, March 29, 1630.

A model of the *Arabella*
WIKIMEDIA COMMONS, BOSTON PUBLIC LIBRARY

17

The trip was as challenging as they had expected. The sea was often rough, the weather cold, and the supplies barely lasted the sixty-six days of the journey. Many suffered from seasickness. Some developed a disease called scurvy caused by a lack of vitamin C, which is found in fresh fruit and vegetables, and one person died of it. Also, the ships were often separated from each other, especially during storms. To add to the travelers' anxiety, they spied a fleet of what looked like pirate ships. Thankfully, as the men prepared for battle, they discovered it was just another English fleet.

Toward the end of May, the *Arabella* came close to its destination: a place the natives had called Naumkeag and the Europeans called Salem, in today's Massachusetts. To celebrate, Winthrop ordered a pause in the journey. The sailors lowered the sails, and some of the men began to fish, catching sixty-seven large cod in less than two hours. It was a timely catch, as they had just used up their supply of salted fish. Some people walked to the shore, where they picked some strawberries. Everyone rejoiced. The new land, Winthrop said, smelled like a garden.

Many people believe that the place where *Arabella* first set anchor in North America was Plum Cove, near Gloucester, Massachusetts.

The next day, Chief Masconomet, head of the Agawam tribe of the Algonquian Native Americans, visited the *Arabella* with one of his men. They stayed on board all day and must have established good relations with Winthrop because, eight years later, Masconomet sold Winthrop some land where the colonists could found a city.

Feeling encouraged, the passengers on the *Arabella* sailed down the coast, arriving in Salem in the early morning of June 12, 1630. They announced their arrival with the blast of a cannon.

Soon, however, the weary travelers realized the reality was much different from what they had anticipated. The winter had been harsher than predicted, and many of the men who had come ahead as scouts had suffered from hunger, illness, and death.

Apart from the local governor and a few others who were able to build houses, most of the early pioneers lived in huts, tents, or caves. Many built their huts in the style of the Native Americans' wigwams. This is a reconstruction of an "English wigwam" in Pioneer Village, Salem, Massachusetts.

NELSON DIONNE SALEM HISTORY COLLECTION, SALEM STATE UNIVERSITY ARCHIVES AND SPECIAL COLLECTIONS, SALEM, MASSACHUSETTS

"We found the Colony in a sad and unexpected condition," Thomas Dudley wrote, "above eighty of them being dead the winter before; and many of those alive weak and sick; all the corn and bread amongst them all hardly sufficient to feed them a fortnight [two weeks]."

It was a disappointment for all and especially shocking for someone like Anne, who had lived in refined English mansions. More than ever before, she realized her life was going to drastically change in ways she was not prepared to face. "I found a new world and new manners at which my heart rose," she wrote many years later.

Anne realized her life was going to change in ways she was not prepared to face.

Since the community at Salem was barely able to provide for their own needs, let alone those of a new group of people, Winthrop and Dudley decided to sail farther south, stopping for some time in a village the native populations called Mishawum, meaning "Great Springs." The English people later renamed it Charlestown after Charles I.

Winthrop, whose son had recently drowned in a boating accident, understood the grief and discouragement of those around him. He also understood more than ever their need to stick together. To reach this goal, he asked everyone to sign a covenant, or sacred agreement, promising to unite "into one congregation, or church, under the Lord Jesus Christ our Head, to obey God's laws, and to love and respect each other, as God shall give us grace."

Anne signed the covenant. As she explained later, by that time she had overcome her initial negative reaction. "After I was convinced it was the way of God," she said, "I submitted to it and joined the church."

Soon after, Winthrop met an Englishman, William Blackstone, who had come to America a few years earlier. Unlike Winthrop's group of recent arrivals, he had managed to build a large and comfortable home on a hilly peninsula called Shawmut (later Boston). There, he had gathered a rich library and planted an apple orchard from seeds he had brought from England. Blackstone convinced Winthrop to move to Shawmut, where there was plenty of clear water to drink and irrigate the fields.

Dudley, instead, tried to keep the community going at Charlestown. But the people who stayed with him continued to die at a fast rate, including Arabella and her husband. By January 1631, he reported two hundred deaths. In a letter to Arabella's mother, he compared their situation to God's tenth plague on Egypt: "There is not a house where there is not one dead, and in some houses many." He blamed it on the lack of heating in winter and sudden heat in summer, as well as the poor diet.

A bronze plaque in Boston's Common (the oldest park in the country) commemorates the time when William Blackstone (on the left in the image) invited John Winthrop to the area where the city of Boston would be founded.

Realizing he had to find a better location, Dudley moved his family away from the coast to an area the Native Americans had cleared some time earlier. Watered by a wide river the natives had called Quinobequin, it promised to be an ideal place to live. The colonists renamed the river Charles, after Charles I, and the place New Towne (later Cambridge).

Anne had barely settled in New Towne when she became very ill. With so many people dying all around her, she thought she would be the next to leave this earth. In a poem, she reminded herself that this life is short and frail, that Christ has won the victory over death, and that there is a much better life ahead.

Fresh Pond, in Cambridge, Massachusetts, had been used by Native Americans for thousands of years for fishing and to draw water.

CHAPTER THREE
A Passion for Writing

The illness lasted for a long time. Even when it passed, Anne found it difficult to walk. Still, she believed the Lord had sent it for her good, and she learned important lessons from it. Eventually, her health improved, and along with a stronger body, she received an answer to a prayer she had repeated for six years: a request for a child. She called her newborn Samuel, after the Old Testament prophet who was an answer to his mother's prayers. This was the beginning of her life as a mother. Between the years 1633 and 1652, she had seven more children.

But Anne would not get too comfortable in New Towne. In 1635, while she was pregnant with her second child, Dudley started to plan a move. His new destination was a strip of coastal land forty

A reconstruction of daily life in the early American colonies. Sewing was an activity women could do together while talking and supporting each other. Besides her mother and sisters, there were probably other women who assisted Anne during her pregnancy, childbirth, and after.

NELSON DIONNE SALEM HISTORY COLLECTION, SALEM STATE UNIVERSITY ARCHIVES AND SPECIAL COLLECTIONS, SALEM, MASSACHUSETTS

miles north of Boston. The natives called it Agawam, meaning "low-lying lands" (later renamed Ipswich by the colonists). As they had done all along, the Bradstreets followed Dudley to keep the family together.

It must have been difficult for Anne to move so far away from the people she had come to know in New Towne and the surrounding area. Forty miles was a long way in those days, and the trip by wagon took about two days over rough roads. It was not a comfortable ride, especially for a pregnant woman, but most families preferred to travel before their babies were born, when they were still safe inside their mothers.

The land around Ipswich was rich with plant, fish, fowl, and water. About thirty other English families were already there. Most likely, the Dudleys and Bradstreets stayed with some of these families while they built their home. By this time, they were probably getting used to this kind of life. As busy as she was, however, Anne kept her passion for reading and writing.

A view of Ipswich River. In one of her poems, Anne said, "I once that lov'd the shady woods so well, now thought the rivers did the trees excel." Both Ipswich and Andover, the next place where Anne lived, had beautiful forests and rivers.

Moving was always difficult.

Woman in period costume cooking at the kitchen fireplace at Whipple House, a historical residence built in Ipswich, Massachusetts, five years after Anne's death.

    The colonists had built a small church in Ipswich, where a pastor named Nathaniel Ward preached every Sunday. Anne was immediately fascinated by Ward's large library, and he was happy to show her his books and talk with her about literature and writing. An author of a couple of books and one more in the making, Ward understood and shared Anne's love for writing.

    With so much encouragement, Anne continued to write. In fact, from the time she arrived in Ipswich to 1648, she wrote more than six thousand lines of poetry—a rare achievement for any poet at that time. Many of her poems were, like Bartas's, long descriptions of historical events. Some were inspired by Bible passages or by the news she heard from England.

Anne's pastor was happy to talk with her about their common love for reading and writing.

But she also wrote short poems about herself, her life, her loved ones, and what she saw all around her. She loved to find the best words to describe her feelings and the comfort she found in the Bible and the world He created. Sitting under a tree by the river, she thought of how trees can be richly dressed in shining autumn colors without feeling the least bit proud. She watched the water "overwhelm" the rocks while the song of a bird perched over her head distracted her from the "thousand fancies buzzing in [her] brain."

Some rocks "overwhelmed" by the water in the Ipswich River, next to the Mills Dam that was built in 1635. This was only a half mile from Anne's house, so it is quite possible that Anne walked here.

If this world is so beautiful, she thought, "how excellent is He that dwells on high, whose power and beauty by His works we know? Sure he is goodness, wisdom, glory, light, That hath this under world so richly dight [dressed]."

Sitting under a tree by the river, Anne thought of the beauty of the God who made it all.

But even though Anne had become attached to Ipswich, she was soon reminded that few things last long in this world. In 1645 Simon, hoping to expand his properties, planned to move his family farther inland, this time to a place Native Americans called Chochichewick, meaning "at the wild, dashing stream" (renamed Andover by the colonists).

Leaving loved ones behind was, once again, very hard. But by that time, Anne's mother had died and her father had moved, so Anne must have been looking forward to reuniting with her sister Mercy, who had moved to Andover with her husband. Anne could count on Mercy to assist her during the birth of her sixth child, who was about to be born.

The Harold Parker State Forest in North Andover gives us an idea of the beauty of nature Anne would have seen every day.

CHAPTER FOUR
A Published Author

Anne must also have been eager to see their new home in Andover. This time, Simon built it before the family moved. With his family safe in Ipswich and a good income from his work as a commissioner and justice of the peace, he was able to hire good laborers and get the best material for the building—the largest they had ever owned. He also made sure the land around it was clear and ready for planting.

If Anne missed her conversations with Ward about poetry and literature, she was soon glad to discover that Mercy's husband, John Woodbridge, shared the same passion. When he traveled to England in 1647, he took a collection of thirteen of Anne's poems with him. There, he found other people who loved her writings as he did. One poem in particular, set as a conversation between Old England and New England, caught the interest of many readers.

For many years, people believed that Parson Barnard House, built around 1715, belonged to Anne Bradstreet and her family. A later document revealed otherwise. Still, it's a good model of colonial homes, except for the columns in front of the door, which became fashionable later on.

It was a difficult time for England. Since 1642, the people had been suffering through a painful civil war (a war between citizens of the same nation). In this case, it was a war between the supporters of Parliament, who wanted the king to respect Parliament's advice as the law demanded, and the supporters of King Charles, who thought that the king had full authority and did not have to consult Parliament. Anne respected the king but was on the side of Parliament.

In Anne's poem, New England, represented by a young woman, talks to her mother, Old England, about the possible cause of these recent problems. Old England admits that she mistreated the

A reconstruction of the Siege of Chester, during the first English Civil War (1645).

preachers who had refused to accept some ceremonies that were forced on them and who had insisted on the pure preaching of the gospel. She remembers with regret how some of these preachers "lost their livings," were imprisoned, or exiled, all because of her laws.

In the end, New England offers her help, but she advises her mother to stop looking to her Roman Catholic past and instead look forward to the new day that had dawned. If she did so, New England said, "days of happiness and rest" will soon follow: "In a while you'll tell another tale."

Many read the poem with much interest because the English people needed encouragement. It was also the first commentary on the English Civil War written by a New Englander. But all the poems included in Anne's collection were interesting, including a long poem in praise of Queen Elizabeth I, a discussion among the four elements (fire, air, water, and earth), and a long poem about the major powers of the ancient world. These poems showed that Anne had a good knowledge of both science and history.

Many people wondered how a woman could write such beautiful and well-informed poems. Some could not believe that Anne did. Anne had predicted all this. She knew that some would say that her hand was better fit for holding a needle than a pen. If her work proved to be good, she said, "they'll say it's stol'n, or else it was by chance."

Title page of the first printing of Anne's poems

WIKIMEDIA COMMONS

This is why Nathaniel Ward, who was in London at the time, wrote a foreword to Anne's book, explaining that she really wrote the poems and did so without neglecting her responsibilities toward her family. In fact, he said, she often wrote at night, while the children were sleeping.

Finally, on July 1, 1650, Anne's thirteen poems were published in London in a booklet entitled *The Tenth Muse Lately Sprung Up in America*. The ancient Greeks believed that there were nine goddesses called muses who inspired literature, science, and art. Possibly, whoever chose the title wanted to introduce Anne as an inspiration for other writers—the tenth muse. The book sold very well.

A PUBLISHED AUTHOR

Anne often wrote at night, when the children were sleeping.

It took a few months before Anne discovered that the book had been published. As she first held her copy, she said she felt a mixture of surprise, joy, and fear because, as most authors do, she noticed many imperfections she would have liked to correct before the book went to press.

As time allowed, she was able to edit her poems and write new ones. And while her first collection of poems included mostly commentaries on current events or reflections on history and science, she now felt free to add personal poems about her life as a wife and mother, the responsibilities that occupied most of her time.

Besides the daily tasks of running her house and caring for her children, she often had to take over her husband's duties while he was traveling, especially when he returned to England to manage his business there and to represent the colony. Still, poetry had become for her a pleasant habit that helped her take her mind off the daily problems and meditate on God's word and ways.

A PUBLISHED AUTHOR

Anne was surprised and a little fearful when she first held her copy of her printed book.

39

CHAPTER FIVE
Joys and Sorrows

Anne felt lonely when her husband was away. Many of her poems were love letters to him, prayers for his safe return, or expressions of thankfulness to God when he came home. Since travel was always dangerous, she often worried about any of her journeying loved ones. For example, when her oldest son, Samuel, went to England in 1657, she heard that another ship along the same route was lost at sea. And while Samuel was in England, another epidemic of smallpox killed several people, including two siblings of the king.

Once, when her husband made the journey to England as representative of New England to the court of King Charles II, she received news that he and his companion had been imprisoned. Thankfully, that was not true, but all this scary news weighed heavily on Anne's mind. In her poems, she reminded herself that what God chooses to do is always best. Then, when her loved ones returned safely, she asked God to help her never to forget His loving-kindness.

Simon Bradstreet

Anne was grateful when her husband returned home safely.

JOYS AND SORROWS

41

By the time Samuel went to England, most of Anne's children had grown up. In a poem, Anne compared them to a bunch of birds leaving the nest. Her second and third children, Dorothy and Sarah, had both married and moved away with their husbands. Simon, Anne's second son, was studying at Harvard, and Dudley, her third, was at school in Ipswich.

Only the youngest three, Hannah, Mercy, and John, were still at home. Anne must have been thankful for their help because her health was often poor. In her poem, she thanked God for keeping and protecting all their children, both at home and while they were away. At a time when important medicines such as antibiotics were not yet available, it was rare for all the children in a family to survive childhood.

The image on this stained-glass window in St. Botolph's Church, Boston, Lincolnshire, England, is inspired by Anne's poem where she describes herself as a mother bird.

But even though God spared Anne the sorrow of losing a child, she soon experienced the pain of losing, one after the other, four of her grandchildren—children of Samuel and his wife, Mercy. The first to die was Elizabeth, at only eighteen months of age. The next, four years later, was Anne, at three and a half years. The same year, the couple's fourth child, Simon, died at only one month of age.

And yet Anne's losses were not over. In 1670 Samuel's wife, Mercy, died after giving birth, and her new baby, born too early, died as well. Mercy was only twenty-eight years old. At that time Samuel was in Jamaica, in the Caribbean, where he was hoping to build a house for his family. But most of his family was now gone.

The poem Anne wrote for her son Samuel, as a message to him, is one of the most moving she ever wrote. At fifty, she was nearing an age considered old at that time. And yet she was alive, while many of her loved ones had died young.

"And live I still to see relations gone," she wrote. First the children, like branches on a tree, had fallen, and now the tree itself: their mother. And Anne, who was so close to them, felt like both tree and branches had crashed down on her. "My bruised heart lies sobbing at the root."

Only one of Samuel and Mercy's children was still alive—five-year-old Mercy, named after her mother. Anne and her husband loved this child like their own and cared for her while Samuel continued his business abroad.

Anne compared the death of her daughter-in-law to the falling of a tree that had already lost four branches. In her sorrow, Anne felt like the tree had crashed down on her.

COLIN-47, FLICKR

Anne and her husband cared for their granddaughter Mercy after her mother died.

JOYS AND SORROWS

In her poems, Anne described these children as flowers that fall before their usual time, two barely in blossom and "the last one a bud." Few people wonder when an old tree starts to rot or when ripe fruit falls to the ground, Anne said, but when "buds new blown…have so short a date," the fact that it's God's hand that guides all "nature and fate" becomes clearer than ever.

And yet knowing that God directs all things was comforting to Anne, who knew that He is "merciful as well as just" and "knows what is best for thee and me." This was a lesson she had learned throughout her life—through every loss, every pain, every illness, every fear. In fact, it was a lesson she had been reminded of just a few years earlier when a fire destroyed her home.

The fire happened in the middle of the night when Anne was asleep. Awakened by cries, she ran outside only to discover it was too late to save the building. All she could do was stand there and watch. Soon, she couldn't even do that. Seeing her home and her belongings go up in flames was just too painful.

Anne could only stand and watch as her house burned to the ground.

Thankfully, no one was hurt, and while the building was destroyed, they were able to save enough supplies to live on for some time while building a new home. Still, Anne found it difficult to pass by the ruins of her old house. Each time she saw it, she remembered everything that had taken place inside: the meals eaten, the stories told, the candles lit, the voices heard. And each time she had to remind herself that everything she had belonged to God and was a gift from Him.

Besides, she had a better home God had prepared in heaven that would never burn down or fall, a place bought for her through "a price so vast as is unknown": the sacrifice of Jesus Christ for her sins. That's why she could end the poem by saying,

> There's wealth enough, I need no more,
> Farewell, my pelf [money], farewell, my store [goods].
> The world no longer let me love,
> My hope and treasure lies above.

CHAPTER SIX
Leaving a Legacy

All these experiences taught Anne many lessons of God's faithfulness, and she could pass them down to her children and grandchildren. When her son Simon asked her to put them in writing, she started a new project. She wrote seventy-seven of these lessons before she died—things she had learned about God and about life and practical things, such as raising children and making good choices.

Many of her examples were taken from everyday things: the best flour for making bread, the danger of eating too much honey, the grinding of corn, the climbing of hops, the fruit on the trees—everything suggested a lesson.

But Anne wanted to leave something else for her children. As her health worsened and death seemed near, she wrote a long letter recounting her life story and everything she had learned. Through her many joys and sorrows, she said, she realized it was when life was hardest that she learned the most: "I have found them the times where the Lord hath manifested the most love to me."

ANNE BRADSTREET

> For my deare Sonne
> Simon Bradstreet
>
> Parents perpetuate their lives in their posterity, and their manners in their imitation. Children do naturally rather follow the failings then the vertues of their predecessors, but I am perswaded better things of you. You once desired me to leaue some thing for you in writing that you might look upon when you should see me no more. I could think of nothing more fit for you, nor of more ease to my selfe, then these short meditations following. Such as they are I bequeath to you; small legacys are accepted by true friends, much more by dutyfull children. I haue avoyded incroaching upon others conceptions because I would leaue you nothing but myne owne, though in value they fall short of all in this kinde, yet I presume they will be better prised by you for the Authors sake. The Lord blesse you wth grace heer, and crown you wth glory heerafter, that I may meet you wth reioyceing at that great day of appearing, wch is the continuall prayer, of
>
> your affectionate mother A B
>
> March 20 1664

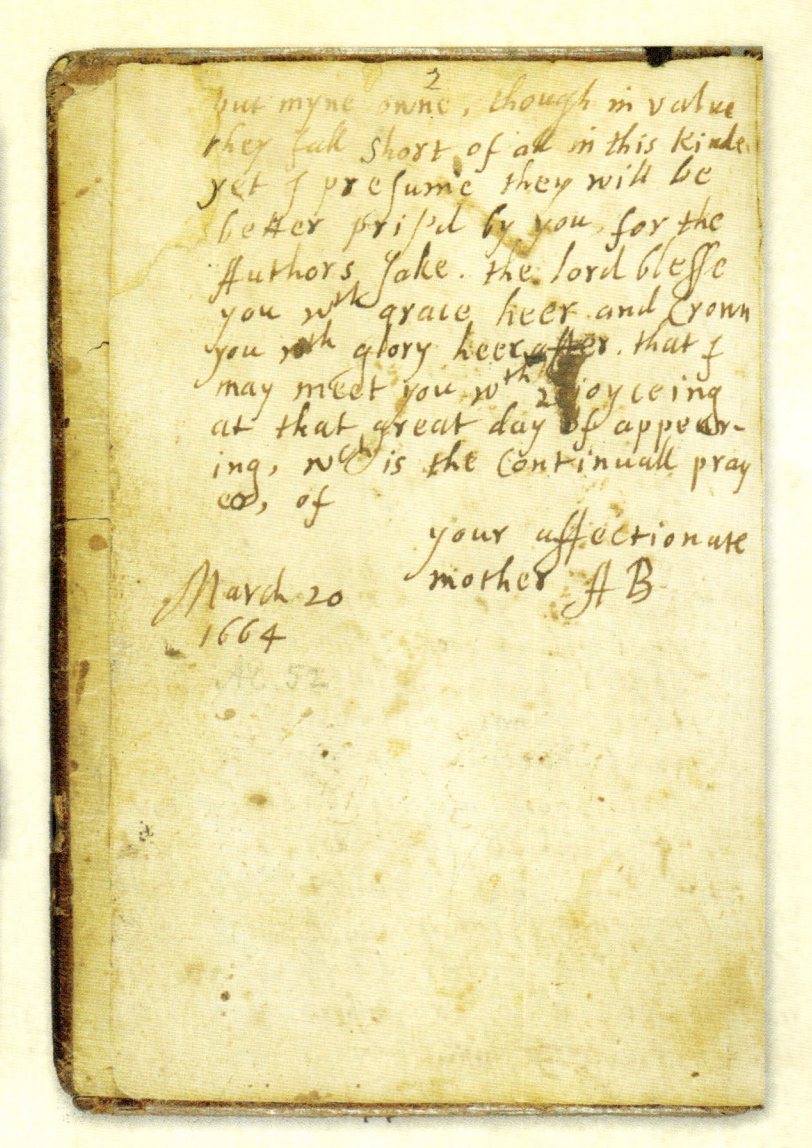

A letter from Anne to her son Simon

MS AM 1007.1. HOUGHTON LIBRARY, HARVARD UNIVERSITY, BY KIND PERMISSION OF THE TRUSTEES OF THE STEVEN MEMORIAL LIBRARY, NORTH ANDOVER, MASSACHUSETTS

Even her doubts had been useful because they had forced her to look for answers. For example, there had been times when she had wondered if there was a God. "I never saw any miracles to confirm me," she said. And how could she know that the ones she had heard about were real? But her reason was enough to tell her that God was real. It was obvious in the wonders she saw in nature, "the vast frame of the heaven and the earth, the order of all things, night and day, summer and winter, spring and autumn, the daily providing for this great household upon the earth, the preserving and directing of all to its proper end."

"But how should I know he is such a God as I worship in Trinity, and such a Savior as I rely upon?" she said. Eventually, she realized that "if God has ever revealed himself, it must be in His work, and this must be it or none." And she knew by experience that God's Word worked on her heart as "no human invention" ever could. Besides, the fact that God's Word has been preserved for centuries in spite of many attempts to destroy it and that it includes so many fulfilled prophecies was proof enough that it was true.

Throughout her life, Anne had many more questions and found more answers. And whenever she had felt discouraged by the problems and false teachings that plagued the church, she remembered that Christ had predicted these things would happen but had also promised to preserve His church. That's why in the end Anne was able to say, "Return, O my soul, to thy rest, upon this Rock Christ Jesus I will build my faith; and if I perish, I perish. But I know all the Powers of Hell shall never prevail against it. I know whom I have trusted and whom I have believed and that he is able to keep that I have committed to his charge."

Anne closed her diary with a wish that if her children ever had to go through similar times of illness, questions, and doubts, they would always remember to look to God, "the same God who hath heard and delivered me, and will do the like for you if you trust in him. And, when he shall deliver you out of distress, forget not to give him thanks, but to walk more closely with him than before. This is the desire of your loving mother."

Anne wrote these words in 1657 after another episode of weakness and fainting. She must have thought it was the end, and yet God kept her on earth fifteen more years. In the meantime, her health continued to get worse until, in 1671, her son Simon described her as "skin and bones." Her last poems show how much she longed for heaven. She died on September 16, 1672, in North Andover, Massachusetts, at the age of sixty, with her husband at her side. Although not all her children could be present at her death, they probably read and reread the letter Anne had written to them.

Anne's children probably read and reread the letter she had written to them.

No one has ever found Anne's grave, but her name continues to be remembered. A new edition of her poems, with the edits and the additions she had prepared, was published in Boston in 1678. This time it bore the simple title Anne had chosen: *Several Poems*. Like the first edition, it became a best seller. Since then, she has influenced many other poets.

In the year 2000, the city of North Andover built a memorial stone for Anne by the entrance of the Old North Parish Cemetery. It quoted a portion of a funeral elegy written in 1672 by John Norton Jr., a friend of Anne's husband: "Mirror of her age, glory of her sex, whose Heaven-born soul, leaving its earthly shrine, chose its native home and was taken to its rest."

Anne's Memorial Stone

Time Line

1612, March – Anne Bradstreet is born in Northampton, England.

1619 – Anne and her family move to Sempringham, Lincolnshire.

1628 – Anne suffers from smallpox. She marries Simon Bradstreet.

1630 – Anne, Simon, and her family travel to the New World. They land at Salem on June 12. They move to nearby Charlestown, then to Cambridge.

1632 – Anne's first son, Samuel, is born.

1635 – Anne and Simon move to Ipswich.

1645 – Anne, Simon, and their children move to Andover.

1650 – *The Tenth Muse* is published in London.

1666 – A fire destroys Anne's home.

1672, September 16 – Anne dies.

1678 – A revised and fuller edition of Anne's works, *Several Poems*, is published in Boston, Massachusetts.

Did you know?

- Francis Higginson, one of the men who went to Salem ahead of Winthrop's fleet, made a list of things he advised all pioneers to carry from England to the New World. It included flour, dried peas, oatmeal, oil, vinegar, butter, cheese, bacon, sugar, pepper, spices, and dried fruit, as well as dishes, silverware, and pots and pans. Other common items were salted beef and fish, cheese, and water. And most families brought their own animals, such as goats, pigs, and chickens. Higginson advised the men to bring both light and warm clothes, a knitted cap, a couple of blankets, enough material to cover whatever they could put into a rough mattress, gardening and woodworking tools, and weapons. The Massachusetts Bay Company, which owned the ships, continued to bring supplies for the colonists to buy. Later colonists were able to get comfortable furniture and other useful items from home or found other immigrants who knew how to build them.

- Most pictures and movies show the early American colonists wearing the same type of clothes. In reality, there was a great variety of styles, just as in Europe, and rich families imported good-quality material. Even those who were not wealthy enjoyed a variety of colors. Most pastors, however, discouraged an excessive display of riches. Some advised their parishioners to avoid wearing gold, silver, and lace. A few forbade them.

- On the *Arabella*, most people slept in large rooms on bunks, hammocks, or mattresses made of straw. Important passengers such as Winthrop, Dudley, Lady Arabella, and their families had small cabins.

- In New England, like in most of Europe, cooking was done in the fireplace, usually in large brass or copper pots. Cornmeal, oatmeal, and stews could all be cooked in the pots, which were also used to make cheese, soap, and candles. There were also spits for roasting meat.

* When Anne arrived in the New World, her money was useful only to buy goods from England. The Native Americans didn't know what to do with coins. They preferred to barter (exchange goods), or they used wampums (traditional beads). Wampum was officially recognized as a currency by Massachusetts Bay Colony in 1650, so that Harvard College accepted it for payment of tuition. European coins became popular later, especially after the colonists began to trade with the West Indies and needed a unified form of payment.

* Colonial children played the usual games of jump rope, hopscotch, leapfrog, tag, and hide-and-seek. As early as 1651, toys and dolls from Europe were sold in the shops of Boston and Salem.

* Winthrop was skilled in medicine, and so were his son John and grandson Wait. Anne's son Simon also became a physician. But medicine was different at that time. Doctors used many herbs and natural remedies that most families already knew about.

* Anne's husband mourned her death for four years—a long time in those days—and moved from Andover to Salem. He later married another Anne, a widow of a captain who had died in war. He served as governor from 1679 to 1686, and again in 1689. His son Dudley took over the family home in Andover.

* In many cultures, both ancient and modern, there have been stories about evil witches casting spells. In 1692 many people in the Massachusetts colonies began to fear witches so much that they started to suspect each other. Both Simon and Dudley Bradstreet tried to calm the panic. Dudley, who was a judge in Andover, held only one witch trial and refused to hold any more. His brother John was actually accused of being a witch simply because a dog barked at him and ran away. All this caused Dudley and John to move to New Hampshire with their families.

- Apart from Dorothy, who died in childbirth soon after her mother's death, all of Anne's children went on to live long lives. Anne's daughter Mercy got married one month after Anne died and had eight children like her mother.

- Both Anne's father and her husband were involved in the founding of Harvard University in New Towne in 1636, and two of Anne's sons, Samuel and Simon, graduated from there. The university was modeled after Cambridge University in England, where many colonists had gotten their education. For this reason, New Towne was soon renamed Cambridge.

    Initially, Harvard was founded to train preachers for the growing colonies. For this reason, besides the main subjects it also taught Greek and Hebrew (the original languages of the Bible). Any man could enroll, as long as they kept its rules, which included that "every one shall consider the main end of his life and studies to know God and Jesus Christ which is eternal life."

- Many seventeenth-century children learned to read and write using a primer—an alphabet book or simple reader. After they learned to read, they were introduced to the Bible. They also studied catechisms, which are summaries of the teachings of the Bible, usually in the form of questions and answers.

    After 1647, Anne would have been able to use the Westminster Shorter Catechism. She probably also used a catechism published by John Cotton in 1646 called *Milk for Babes*. Between 1687 and 1690, a publisher in Boston printed the first primer written specifically for the colonies in New England.

    The *New England Primer* included a biblical ABC, from A ("In Adam's fall we sinned all") to Z ("Zaccheus he did climb the tree his Lord to see"). Other entries included "B—Thy life to mend this book attend"; "H—My book and heart shall never part"; "K—Kings should be good, not men of blood"; and "T—Time cuts us all, both great and small."

    The primer also included the first edition of this famous children's prayer:

Now I lay me down to sleep,
I pray Thee, Lord, my soul to keep;
If I should die before I wake,
I pray Thee, Lord, my soul to take.

* John Cotton moved to Boston, Massachusetts, in 1633 and became the second pastor of the Boston church, so Anne would have been able to hear his sermons there. In 1654 John Cotton's son Seaborn married Anne's daughter Dorothy (he was twenty years old, and she was eighteen). Seaborn, so named because he was born during the journey to New England, went on to become a pastor like his father. He and Dorothy had nine children.

* Some seventeenth-century English names can sound very odd to us today. Some examples include From-Above, Free-Gift, More-Fruit, Hoped-For, Sorry-for-Sin, Praise-God, Die-Well, What-God-Will, Job-Raked-Out-of-the-Ashes, Resolved, Return, Believe, Wait, Remember, Unite, Dust, or simply Thanks.

A widowed mother called her son Father-gone. Two siblings on the *Mayflower* (the ship that brought some Puritans to America in 1620) were named Love and Wrestling. Children who were born during the journey across the ocean were often given names that reminded them of that occasion, such as Seaborn, Oceanus, and Peregrine (meaning "pilgrim," someone on a journey toward a destination).

Some names were particularly long, such as If-Christ-Had-Not-Died-for-Thee-Thou-Hadst-Been-Damned (he later changed his name to Nicholas) or Jesus-Christ-Came-into-the-World-to-Save.

And while common Bible names such as John, Samuel, Joseph, Sarah, and Hannah were always popular, some parents chose more unusual ones, such as Zurishaddat, meaning "the Almighty is my rock" or Mehetabel ("God benefits").

These odd names, as entertaining as they might sound today, were actually very rare, even in those times.

* Anne never mentioned any contact with the Native Americans, but they were living all around her. The European settlers had mixed reactions to the Native Americans. Some appreciated them, while some viewed them as

uncivilized and dangerous. Some recognized their ownership of the land and bought it from them at a fair price, and others thought the land was up for grabs. A pastor named Roger Williams spoke out for the rights of the Native Americans and eventually founded a separate colony in Rhode Island where he could make sure those rights were respected.

Another pastor, John Eliot, had a special desire to bring the gospel to the Native Americans in his area. To do so, he began to study the Massachusett or Wampanoag language under the guidance of a young native, Cockenoe, who had been captured in war. Cockenoe spoke both English and Wampanoag, so he was able to assist Eliot in the translation of the whole Bible in that language. Eliot's efforts were hindered by armed conflicts between the Europeans and the Native Americans, especially King Philip's War (1675–1678).

In any case, the European settlers could be thankful to the Indians for building a large network of roads throughout most of the land. The roads were small and unpaved but good enough for travel on horseback and in small carts. Also, the Native Americans had burned much of the overgrowth to allow travelers to cross the large forests.

From Anne's Pen

UPON THE BURNING OF OUR HOUSE

In silent night when rest I took,
For sorrow near I did not look,
I awakened was with thundering noise
And pitiful shrieks of dreadful voice.
That fearful sound of "Fire!" and "Fire!"
Let no man know is my desire.

I, getting up, the light did spy,
And to my God my heart did cry
To strengthen me in my distress
And not to leave me succorless.
Then, coming out, saw a space,
The flame consume my dwelling place.

And when I could no longer look,
I blessed His name that gave and took,
That laid my goods now in the dust.

Yea, so it was, and so it was just.
It was His own, it was not mine;
Far be it that I should repine.

He might of all justly bereft
But yet sufficient for us left.
When by the ruins often I passed
My sorrowing eyes aside did cast
And here and there the places spy
Where often I sat and long did lie.

Here stood that trunk, and there that chest;
There lay that store I counted best.
My pleasant things in ashes lie,
And them behold no more shall I.
Under your roof no guest shall sit
Nor at your table eat a bit.

---

* From *The Poems of Mrs. Anne Bradstreet (1612–1672): Together with Her Prose Remains*, edited by Frank Easton Hopkins, 1897. Slightly edited into modern English for young readers.

No pleasant tale shall ever be told
Nor things recounted done of old.
No candle ever shall shine in thee,
Nor bridegroom's voice ever heard shall be.
In silence ever shall you lie.
Adieu! Adieu! All is vanity.

Then I began my heart to chide:
And did your wealth on earth abide?
Did you fix your hope on moldering dust?
The arm of flesh did you make your trust?
Raise up your thoughts above the sky,
That dunghill mists away may fly.

You have a house on high erect
Framed by that mighty Architect,
With glory richly furnished,
Stands permanently although this be fled.
It's purchased and paid for too
By Him who has enough to do.

A prize so vast as is unknown,
Yet by His gift is made your own.
There's wealth enough. I need no more.
Farewell, my money, farewell, my store.
The world no longer let me love.
My hope and treasure lies above.

Acknowledgments

My deepest thanks go to Dr. Francis J. Bremer, editor of the *Winthrop Papers* and professor emeritus of history at Millersville University of Pennsylvania, for taking the time out of his busy schedule to read and correct this book. And I am grateful to Dr. Michael Haykin, chair and professor of church history and director of the Andrew Fuller Center for Baptist Studies at the Southern Baptist Theological Seminary, who referred me to Dr. Bremer and who is always ready to offer encouragement.

As usual, I thank everyone at Reformation Heritage Books for their unwavering support; my faithful illustrator, Matt Abraxas, and map artist, Tom Carroll; everyone who has provided photos; and my patient husband, Tom, who is always willing to listen to my discoveries. This book would not have been possible without you.